The Danger of Not Waiting on God

Carolyn B. James

ISBN 978-1-64569-706-0 (paperback)
ISBN 978-1-64569-707-7 (digital)

Copyright © 2019 by Carolyn B. James

All rights reserved. No part of this publication may be reproduced, distributed, or transmitted in any form or by any means, including photocopying, recording, or other electronic or mechanical methods without the prior written permission of the publisher. For permission requests, solicit the publisher via the address below.

Christian Faith Publishing, Inc.
832 Park Avenue
Meadville, PA 16335
www.christianfaithpublishing.com

Printed in the United States of America

Ignoring Warning Signs

In the word of God, we find that Jesus used many methodologies basically, to bring out different principles of the scriptures. In other words, Jesus used natural metaphors to bring out the spiritual.

I'm going to take this opportunity, to depict, how we can easily ignore warnings signs, both spiritual and natural. Think about it, have you ever had or experienced a sharp pain in a certain part of your body? Absolutely, we all have. When we feel pain, what does that usually indicate? Pain in the body is an indication that something is wrong. If that pain persists, you go and see a physician. Why? Because you had a warning sign. Failure to pay attention to the pain could be serious or deadly. If you are driving on the road and you come to a sign that says, "Slow down construction ahead," what do you think will happen if you don't "heed" that warning sign? You are likely to get pulled over by a police officer and get yourself a nice ticket. There are consequences when we don't obey the laws of the land. Well, if we have to obey man's laws, or suffer a penalty behind it, what about when we disobey God's word?

The same thing applies, for those of us that are "blood-bought believers" of Christ Jesus. There are certain standards that God holds his children to. But in order to know what God is requiring from us, we must stay under good leadership so you can be taught the word of God, what God is saying concerning our lives. To know God is to know "*his*" word so we don't fall "prey" to our adversary, the devil. Regardless of how anointed you are, how long you been saved, you gotta stay in the "Word of God." Keep your hips in the "ark of safety," the house of prayer, if not you are destined to fall.

Stay alert, watch, and pray! Don't be tricked.

Don't lose your focus on the things of God, don't be lovers of pleasures, more than lovers of God. Yes, when God, saved us, "*he*" made us free. Don't get it twisted, God, didn't make us free to live like the devil, but live unto, "him." That's why in God's word, "he" specifically, tells us to walk in the spirit, that we not fulfill the lust of our flesh! When you walk in the flesh, you are no longer walking in the "Spirit of God." The Holy Ghost will definitely, warn us when we get off course. It is our responsibility to listen and be attentive to what God is saying, and showing us. The worst scenario is to walk in disobedience and failure to pay attention to the warning signs. God always sends a warning before destruction.

Don't ignore the "warning signs." Remember there are consequences for what we do, whether good or bad. We serve such a loving God; "*he*" loves us past our "sin." All God asks is that we confess, repent, turn away from our "sin."

Whatsoever God has promised you, whether it is a mate, a new home, a car, healing, trust "him" to do what "he" says. God is always faithful to *his* "Word." He's faithful even when we're not. Don't risk the promises of God for the lies, of the "enemy." You've gone through too much to not trust God. Whatever God has "promised" you, it shall come to pass. Trust and believe. When the devil whispers "lies" concerning your future, remind that devil of God's promise concerning your life. The devil is a lying wonder, there's no "truth" in him. Don't be moved by your adversary, the devil. Keep him under your feet.

Can I just encourage you to stay in the race? Don't give up. Hold fast to those things you have been taught. Don't waver in the faith, but stand strong in the Lord. If you are one that happened to have fallen from the faith, get back *up*! You don't have to stay where you are, God loves you!

Don't allow the enemy to beat you up with your past. You can "begin again."

CHAPTER 2

Ignoring Warning Signs

God loves us so much so that when we fall from grace, if we confess our faults and repent, he is lawful and just to forgive us. He (God) wipes the slate clean and our sins are no longer remembered. Isn't that "good news?" Unfortunately, there are people that are bound by the devil, so much that when they get delivered, they fall back into "sin" again. These are people with a great call of God upon their lives. Sin will blind us to the fact that you are willing to lose your soul for a life of pleasure. The Word of God tells us, "What does it profit a man to gain the whole world and lose his own soul." The devil knows his time ain't long, so of course his job is to deceive as many of the children of God as he can. This is why we must give ourselves to fasting and prayer, studying and meditating on God's word.

It's imperative that we as believers in Christ know the Word of God. Let the Word of God become "grounded" and "rooted" on the inside of you. That's your ammunition against that "devil." We got to get suited up with the armor of God. We are soldiers in God's army. Whose army are you in? If you belong to God's army, you gotta fight the good fight. We fight in the Spirit, not in our "flesh." The weapons of our "warfare is not carnal," but mighty through the pulling down of "strongholds." We cannot please God in our "flesh."

God gets no glory out of our lives walking in carnality. Blessing and cursing can't come out of the same mouth neither can sweet water nor bitter water come out the same fountain. There has to be a change, people of God! There must be a difference, sinners can no longer tell who's saved and who isn't because the church is now embracing things of the world. There has to be a difference church. God*'s* word has not and will not change.

God*'s* Word is the same yesterday, today, and forever. That's the Word of God. We might as well make it up in our minds that we are either going to serve God or the devil. We can't be "halted" between two opinions. We either serve one or the other. God is calling for "real people." *So*, just know if you are saved, but yet cussing, partying, drinking, fornicating, doing whatever you want, you need deliverance. God can deliver you, but you gotta want it "for real."

God is such a "gentleman," he's not gonna break our will. Now, there is a flip side to God. *If* we insist on doing things our way, making a mockery out of *"him."* Oh, he knows how to humble you. We best humble ourselves than have God do it.

One thing for sure, where sin abides God will not dwell. I'm a witness. When I fell back into sin, honestly, I never thought it would happen to me, but it did. I was under a very strict teaching at this time. I truly loved God and was living holy as best as I knew how. We were taught you couldn't have a boyfriend, and I didn't. It was during the period of God, transitioning me from where I was under a female pastor. She was very firm and a very strict teacher. So when I left I felt really free, but at the same time feeling vulnerable and insecure. The devil set me up. I end up meeting the guy I dated in high school. We meet, exchanged numbers. I was excited because I actually wanted a male friend just to talk to. Unfortunately, he had other things on his mind. When I told him beforehand what wasn't going to happen, we'll have dates, he'll later cancel. I knew the real reason he did it. It was obvious he had a different agenda, but I continue to talk with him. I finally fell in the snare of the enemy. The very thing

THE DANGER OF NOT WAITING ON GOD

I said wouldn't happen, happened. Trust me I learned a very valuable lesson. Never say what you won't do! We're no match for the enemy.

It's only with God's help that we're only able to escape the tactics of the enemy. Praise God, I couldn't stay in my mess. I repented and turned back to God. So glad I did!

CHAPTER 3

Warning Signs, "Pay Attention"

The worst thing we can do is "*ignore*" the warning signs that God allows us to discern. Take for instance in the natural, if you are traveling the interstate, and you are to exit off 104 going to McCullough, Al. There's a sign warning you to take exit 100 instead because construction is being done on exit 104, that road is now closed. Well, it's up to you to pay attention and take heed to the warning sign, *failure* to do so will cause you to enter a place that's no longer accessible. Now, you have to turn around and re-route in order to get back on exit 100. Time lost because you didn't pay attention. You were determined to see whether or not you can still take the exit you come to be familiar with. Only to find out the road is really "*closed.*"

    A lot of things we can avoid in the road if we heed the signs along the road. "Don't detour!" Stay on course, don't become distracted. Once you lose your focus, you also lose your discernment. Be sensitive to the Holy Spirit. It will not mislead you, it will guide you in all "*truth.*" To be sensitive to the spirit means to become intimate with your God.

    One thing for sure the devil will *never* do is warn you of any danger that lies ahead of you. God loves us so much that he sends warning before destruction, but we must pay attention. The devil comes to "steal, kill, and destroy!" He doesn't care anything about you, especially if you are a blood-bought believer; he wants to kill you. He doesn't want what God has impregnated you with to be birthed. He wants to abort what you are carrying, you are a "threat" to the devil. Don't allow the enemy to cause you to travail before time. "Keep your focus."

Don't become the devil's "*prey.*"

CHAPTER 4

Warning Signs, "Pay Attention"

"Be sober, be vigilant (watchful); because your adversary the devil, is as a roaring lion, walketh about seeking whom he may devour" (1 Peter 5:8, KJV). The devil is cunning and he's very crafty, he sits and he strategizes how he will attack. The word of God tells us, "Lest Satan should get an advantage of us: we are not ignorant of his devices" (2 Corinth. 2:11).

Unfortunately, a lot of times being saved as single women, the devil will come at a time of loneliness. A time when you become vulnerable, now here comes that lying devil whispering in your ear, "Oh, if I just only had a male companion, you know somebody to dine out with, or go to the movies with." Now you're trying to convince yourself that's all you want. Maybe, that's what you truly believed, beloved. But guess who else is sitting on the sideline, listening at your request, *yep*, that's right, the devil. Now, unless you are able to strategically discern, when God's hand is on a thing or when it's the *devil*, you will be deceived. Don't be tricked! The devil will come dressed in a three-piece suit, looking good, smelling good, telling you all the wonderful things you haven't heard in a long time. You can become so spiritually blind that you will think this man is "*god sent*" when he is actually an assignment sent from "*hell.*"

I have learned that when a person wants satisfaction, they don't want advice. How do you know? Well I'm glad you asked, take for instance you are saved and this unsaved man comes along telling you everything he thinks you want to hear and see in a man. Another sister in the Lord comes along and says, "Sis Watermelon, that man is not for you." Why? Because she's able to discern some things about him that you now are blinded to. Oh, but in Sis Watermelon's mind that sister just jealous and don't want to see you with anybody good.

CHAPTER 5

Warning Signs, "Don't Ignore"

The devil got you just where he wants you. He's now sitting along the sidelines saying, "I got cha!" It's easy to get off the straight and narrow path, if you don't keep your eyes on the prize, which is "Christ Jesus." I don't care how anointed you are, how long you've been saved, if we don't stay prayed up, be steadfast in the word of God, stay around some strong saints, fast and seek God's face, you are destined to fall.

Why? Because now your focus is on how to please a man, where you once had an active prayer life, it's little to none now. This joker is telling you all kinds of lies because he has a different agenda from what you have. If he ever gets you to let your guard down, oh baby, it's a done deal. Once that seed is sown into you, you now become one flesh, and now you have taken on his sinful nature. *Now*, he doesn't have to pursue you so hard for sex cause now your flesh is craving for him as well. Oh, the script has flipped. Now, you're calling him cause your flesh is cutting up and you need him to handle his business. Everything you've been taught is now, non-effective. "Submit yourselves therefore to God. Resist the devil, and he will flee from you" (James 4:7). The word of God also tells us when we are drawn out in our lust. "Don't say you are tempted of God: for God cannot be tempted with evil. Neither he tempted any man" (James 1:13, KJV).

When we walk in the flesh, that sinful nature, we mind the things of the flesh. In other words, whatever that flesh craves for, you are now fulfilling it. Where you stop going to clubs and using all sorts of profanity, now you have opened up yourself to other demonic spirits. Evil spirits are real!

CHAPTER 6

Warning Signs, "Don't Be Deceived"

> Then goeth he (unclean spirit) and take with himself seven other spirits more wicked than himself, and they enter in and dwell (live), there: and the last state of that man (you), is worse than the first. (Matthew 12:45)

Don't be deceived, we are no match for the enemy.

The devil's intentions are to destroy you. He doesn't care who he has to use to do it. Oh, but the good news my sister, you don't have to stay where you are, we got an advocate with the Father, his name is Jesus. He's always making intercessions to our heavenly Father on our behalf.

There's *not* anything too bad or good that you or I have done or can do to stop our God from loving us. Does that give us license to continue to sin? Of course not! "What shall we say then? Shall we continue in sin, that grace may abound? God forbid. How shall we that are dead to sin, live any longer therein?" (Romans 6:1).

Understand, beloved one of Christ, when we received Jesus as our Lord and Savior, we now belong to him, we are no longer of our own, we have been redeemed by the "*blood of the lamb*" and we now belong to *him*, why? Because he purchased us, he bought us back from a world of sin, that we might be free to serve him and not sin. I can imagine somebody saying nobody can live free of sin, we've all sinned and fell short of God's glory. That's true, but dear hearts, once you become saved, sanctified, and filled with the Holy Spirit, you now become a new creature in Christ Jesus. Your body now belongs to Christ, not man. We, as children of God, should not make it a practice to "*sin.*" Does this mean you or I won't fall or error? Of course you will, but know that God has given us away of escape. He will not let us be "tempted" more than we are able. And, just in case you are tempted or have sinned, confess it, repent, and turn away from it. Jesus is lawful and just to forgive us of all our unrighteousness. He loves us that much!

CHAPTER 7

Warning Signs,
"Don't Be Deceived" Part 2

Yes, beloved of Christ, he does indeed love us so much that he will give us a way to escape temptations. Meaning, we don't have to yield unto temptation, unless we choose to. We will be tempted, make no mistake about it. Jesus himself was also tempted by the devil.

Did Jesus yield unto Satan? Absolutely *not*! Sin doesn't become sin until we actually give into it. Some people may be inclined to disagree, that's fine, you are entitled to your opinion.

Here's a scenario for you: if I had thoughts of robbing a bank but never followed through with it, the police can't come and arrest me on a thought, can he? Only until I commit the crime. Then and only then do the police officers have grounds to arrest me. The enemy loves planting this seed in the believer's mind, "Oh, God is a forgiving God." Yes, indeed he is. "Oh well, God already knows I got a problem with my flesh." That's true God knows all things, he knows our beginning and our *end*. The fact of the matter is we are still without "excuse." "This I say then walk in the spirit, and ye will not fulfill the lust of the flesh" (Galatians 5:16, KJV). We as children of God cannot take on the world's form, doing worldly things, and please God.

Absolutely *not*, you either love one (God) or hate the other (the *devil*), but you cannot serve them both. If a man is married and he has a mistress on the side, whoever he spends most of his time with, that's who he wants. There's no way a husband can love his wife and allow his house to go lacking. If he's not spending his time and money at home that means he is spending it on something or someone else. But, he cannot love them both. It's either love or lust.

Don't be deceived. How do you think our God feels when we are unfaithful to him?

CHAPTER 8

Warning Signs,
"Our Unfaithfulness to God"

The word of God tells us plainly that if you love him, you keep his commandments. We, the church, are styled as the "bride of Christ." Whenever we sin in this body, we also sin against God. Our bodies now belong to him.

> What? Know ye not that your body is the temple of the Holy Ghost which is in you. You are of God, and ye are not your own. For ye are bought with a price: therefore glorify God, in your body, and in your spirit, which is God's. (1 Corinthians 6:19–20)

Now, when we belong to God that means we can't use our temple or our bodies for fornication, sex outside of marriage. Why? If you are saved, your life is no longer your own. We just can't do what we wanna, when we wanna, in this body. *Why?* Because it is now the place where God spirit dwells.

When we continue to sin against God with our bodies, we put him to open shame. It's like a husband or wife discovering his or her spouse has been cheating on them. Where sin dwells, the spirit of God no longer dwells. God does not dwell in an unclean temple. Secondly, being unfaithful to God, is like a husband or wife choosing to separate when they learn of the infidelity during their marriage. They have the choice to reconcile or divorce. Just like we, as believers, have the choice to repent and be reconciled back unto God, and he will receive us back as his own. He loves us so much that he's willing to wipe the slate clean as though nothing happened. The danger of it all is when we fail to *"repent"* and continue on in our sins. As the word of God says he is a jealous God and he knows how to get your attention. Trust me!

"Those God loves he chasten" (Proverbs 3:12).

CHAPTER 9

Warning Signs, "Lies of the Enemy"

The enemy will come to us at a time when we are vulnerable, lonely, frustrated, not praying, and definitely when we are not watching. The word of God says Satan comes as a roaring lion seeking whom he may devour. Satan's whole objective is to catch the people of God off guard. That's how we fall "*prey*" to the lies and the tactics of the "*enemy.*"

The enemy doesn't care how anointed you are, how much you speak in tongues, or how long you have been saved, he wants to *destroy* you. We as single, saved, Holy Ghost-filled women must be careful that we don't allow ourselves to become his target. It's imperative that we pray and ask God for a saved mate. Then, we must be willing to "wait" and "trust" God to give us the mate we need and desire. So many times we as women of God do not want to *wait*… that's how we end up marrying the wrong mate or our assignment.

We allow the lies of the enemy to get into our ears, whispering how we'll never get married. "Look how long you've been saved, and you're still not married. Girl, you're getting older and after a while you'll be too old to enjoy a husband." All lies of the enemy. Then what you go and do, Sara, you decide you'll help God out by taking the initiative to date an unsaved man. Oh, you have fallen right into Satan's trap. The worst thing you can do as a saved woman, get hooked up with an unsaved man with the concept you can change him. Don't be deceived the way I was. Unfortunately, I had to learn the hard way. That's why I'm trying to save you, so that you don't make the same mistake I did. Nine times out of ten, they don't want your God, they may go to church with you a couple of times, if only to try and convince you they really want you.

CHAPTER 10

Warning Signs, "Lies of the Enemy" Part 2

Some men will do whatever to impress and convince you they are serious about you. Trust me, they have an agenda, beloved, and that's to get you to lower your standards. Once you do, you can forget it. It's gonna be really hard to try and witness to someone you are intimate with. Why would they want to listen to you now when his needs are being met? That lying demon will show you all the things he think you wanna see in a man and all the sweet nothings he thinks you want to hear. All lies.

You deserve so much better. If you allow them to sleep with you, I can almost guarantee you, they are intimate with someone else. Don't be deceived thinking you got it going on like that because you don't. Don't lose your soul over a few minutes of pleasure. There is a penalty when we sin against our bodies, we sin against God. Confess it and turn away. God gives us a time and a space to *repent*, it's up to us to take *heed*. Remember, the devil comes to steal, kill, and destroy, but God comes that we may have life. The wages of sin, is death, the gift of God is eternal life. Choose life. There's a saying that says, "Sin will keep you longer than you wanna stay, cost you more than you're willing to pay." This is true, after all, sin tastes good, looks good, and feels good, but it's not worth "eternal judgment" or "damnation."

God, don't want us being unequally yoked with unbelievers. "Can two walk together, except they be agreed?" (Amos 3:3). Don't be fooled. Where there is light, darkness must flee. And even if he agrees to marry you, it won't last. Only what God joins together and ordains will last. "What God, has joined together let no man put asunder" (Matthew 19:6).

CHAPTER 11

Know Who You Are in Christ Jesus

It's important that we as a body of believers know who we are and what God says concerning us. Satan is the father of lies, there's no truth in him. The only truth is God's word. The devil counts on us being ignorant of God's word, that's how he gets a foothold over us. "Unless Satan gets an advantage, we're not ignorant of his devices" (2 Corinthians 2:11). Don't allow the enemy to deceive you with his "lies." We are the "righteousness of Christ," children of the Most High God. Do you know that we are adopted into the royal family of Christ; we are heirs and joint heirs. Therefore, we the children of the Most High God have the rights to our heavenly Father's inheritance.

Sisters, we represent "royalty," act and carry yourselves as such. No longer should we fall for the lies and tactics of the enemy. Tell yourself, "No longer, will I settle, but I shall have all God says I can have. I am who God says I am." *Believe* what the Bible says about you, "you are fearfully and wonderfully made" (Psalm 139:14). Whenever the devil whispers lies in your ear about you not being pretty enough, smart enough, not able to articulate well, you don't fit in, "*all lies!*" Did you hear me? Remind that lying devil what God's words say concerning you. God is "*truth*" and *he* doesn't tell lies.

Know God's word and what he says concerning you. The word of God is our sword and our shield against the devil's tactics and strategies. The word of God says we must be wise as a serpent, harmless as a dove. We gotta stay in the Word of God, that's our only truth. That's the only way to defeat the devil and his lies, with God's *truth*, his Word.

CHAPTER 12

Know Who You Are in Christ Jesus Part 2

When you truly know who you are in Christ Jesus, the devil knows he can't intimidate you. Why? Because you know who God has called you to be. When, you have that assurance from God of who you are and what he has called you to be, stand boldly on it. Don't allow the *devil* to make you feel less than what God called you to be. Walk in the vocation God has called you to. In other words, stay in your lane. I don't care if you share a platform with someone that knows all Hebrew and Greek. Give what God has given you.

The devil will try to bring a spirit of intimidation upon you or make you feel inferior. Again, know who God has called you to be. Don't try to mimic or imitate someone else so that you can look or sound good. Remember, you were chosen and divinely designed by God. You are uniquely crafted from any other. Why would you wanna act like someone else? Be who God has called you to be, for he knows the plans concerning your life.

Sometimes when we lack self-esteem and that confidence, it's hard to see yourself the way God and others do. People can tell you all day, "Oh, you're powerful," "Oh, you are really anointed," etc., but you gotta know what God has invested in you. Exemplifying meekness can be a good thing because it indicates your humility in the Lord. Never allow people to build you up by telling you how great they think you are. These same people that build you up will be the very ones to tear you down. Always give God back his *glory*. Stay *humble* and *meek* before him, and "*he*" will exalt you in due time. Not people!

CHAPTER 13

Stay Focused, "Don't Venture off Straight Street"

When Peter and the rest of the disciples were aboard the boat, they saw what they thought was a ghost, and Jesus said to them to fear not.

Peter replied, "Lord, if it's you, bid me to come to you."

The Lord said, "Come, Peter."

He then got out of the boat, walking toward Jesus. But when he saw how boisterous the wind was, he became afraid and began to sink, then he cried out, "*Lord*, save me!" (Matthew 14:25–31).

It was not until Peter took his eyes off Jesus that he began to notice how boisterous the wind was, he then begins to panic and sink!

What am I saying? Whenever we lose focus on the things of God, we begin to sink back into the lustful things that God delivered us once from. Trust me, there's no way, "child of God," that you can remain spiritual-minded if you're not feeding your spiritual man with the word of God. If you don't feed your natural body with physical food, you will become sick, begin to lose weight, and have health problems. Why? Because you are not eating properly and getting the proper nutrients. When you don't pray, spend time in your word, spend time before God, you're getting ready to venture off the road called straight street. Now, your flesh is waking up because you've been starving your spiritual man, now you're walking in carnality. We cannot please God in the flesh. He that walketh in the flesh does mind the things of the flesh. Now, your focus is off doing the things pleasing unto God, now it's about pleasing your flesh.

Now, you're dressing and acting like the world. Where you were once faithful in the church, now you are rarely seen. Whenever you do come, now you take a sit in the back pew, the devil now got you thinking people are judging you, but the truth of the matter is you are feeling convicted.

That's what sin will do.

CHAPTER 14

When You Lose Your Focus on God

I often time used to wonder how people that used to be on fire for God no longer act like they knew him. That's what happens when you start walking and fulfilling the lust of your flesh. Your flesh began craving for things that are ungodly. There's a war within our members, the flesh war against the spirit, and the spirit against the flesh. The scriptures say they are contrary, one toward the other.

When we lose our focus, we make bad choices that we ordinarily wouldn't do if we stay focused on the things of God. We cannot please God walking in the flesh. When you find yourself comfortable cussing, fornicating, partying, comfortable hanging out with unsaved people, you have *fallen* from the faith. The only time we as believers should be hanging out with the world is when you're trying to win them to Christ. He that is a friend to the world is enmity against God, James 4:4 (KJV). In other words, we become enemies to God. You begin serving God and the devil too.

The wages of sin is death, the gift of God is eternal life. There's a penalty when we sin against God in our bodies. Our bodies are the temples of God, for the Holy Ghost to dwell or abide. The Bible says if we defile his temple, him he shall destroy 1 Corinthians 3:17 (KJV).

God has many ways of destroying us. God, doesn't take pleasure in destroying us. "If we insist on being disobedient and continuing in our sin rather than "repent," we will die spiritually, then a natural death.

God gives us a time and a space to "*repent.*" He's faithful and just to forgive us of all our unrighteousness. He'll wipe the slate clean, the choice is ours. Get your focus back!

CHAPTER 15

When You Lose Your Focus on God Part 2

Let's be clear, beloved, that although God is a God of *love*, he's also a God of wrath. God, will not allow me nor you to continue to bring him to open shame. When we continue to walk in a spirit of disobedience, then God, our heavenly father, will chastise us. Much like when you disobeyed your earthly parents they discipline you, not because they were being mean but because of their love for you. If a parent continues to allow their children to disobey them and never disciplines them, their children will grow worse and worst. This is how our heavenly father feels. God says in his word that whomever "*he*" loves, "*he*" chastises.

We ought to be grateful and thankful that God loves us so much that he doesn't want us continuing in our sins. The choice is ours, whether we "*heed*" our God's warning or not. Unfortunately, there have been many powerful saints of God that didn't make it back. Don't gamble with your salvation. When the grace of God is on your life, you cannot get away with continuing in sin. Why? Because such a conviction will come upon you. What you once took pleasure in doing is no longer so pleasurable now. When you truly love and fear God, you can't continue in sin. There's a seed of righteousness planted inside us. You ever wondered why some people fall into sin and don't seem to get convicted? And, the least little thing you do that's not right, you become convicted, to the point you cannot continue in your mess. When God's hand is upon your life, you cannot get away with doing what's not right in the sight of God. God has a seal, marked upon the foreheads of his chosen people. You can't deny "*him*," your speech will betray you. The devil knows when you are in a place you have no business in.

CHAPTER 16

Chosen, but Running from the Calling of God

Ain't that something, you can't even go up in a club without being recognized by the devil. Aren't you saved? What are you doing in here, girl, you know you don't have any business in here. God may allow that one person to be in a specific place to remind you that you don't belong there. You can run, but you can't hide from the call of God.

True story, it was this minister, a very powerful and anointed woman of God. There was talk that she would be seen in a club and when she would be on the dance floor, she would look like she's shouting. At first I didn't believe it because of who she was until this person I knew really well that wasn't saved confirmed the same thing.

So, I don't care what we think we might be doing in secret, God has a way of exposing us openly. *He's* omnipresent, he's everywhere at one time. His eyes are in every corner, beholding the good and the evil. There's nothing that God doesn't know. Isn't it funny how we will fear the preacher more than God? Now, God's eyes are constantly on us, night and day he hears, sees, and knows all things. The minute we hear our pastor is coming over, you're trying to clean up your act cause you don't want him to know what's really going on with you.

THE DANGER OF NOT WAITING ON GOD

It's right to reverence your leader, but we shouldn't fear them more than God. I think if we will have that same concept, realizing that God is watching and monitoring all that we do, whether good or bad, we'll be less likely to sin willfully against God. Let's be mindful that God's eyes are upon us, that *he* neither sleeps nor slumbers. And we must answer to him for every deed done in our bodies. Our bodies belong to God, whose temple are ye?

CHAPTER 17

Grateful for God's Grace and Mercy

So grateful for God's grace and "*his*" mercy concerning my life. Thank God he didn't give me my just reward every time I sinned or walked in the spirit of disobedience. Thank God for repentance, thank him for his forgiveness concerning my life. We are so blessed to serve a God that loves us past our sin. He's always there waiting with outstretched hands to receive us back unto himself. There's no "sin" too great that he won't forgive us from, with the exception of blaspheme of the Holy Ghost. His word declares, "He that shall blaspheme against the Holy Ghost hath no forgiveness, but is in danger of eternal damnation" (Mark 3:29).

The worst scenario is to know we are walking in error and to justify our wrong. Well, God knows I have a problem with my flesh, God knows I'm not perfect, he's a forgiving God. All this is true, yet we are still without "*excuse.*" He has given us a way of escape. Pray that you enter not into temptation, and just in case you do, "stop," repent, and turn from your sinful ways.

Get back on track, return back to your first love, Christ Jesus. He wants to be first or nothing in our lives, after all he's a jealous God. He doesn't want us putting nothing before him. God wants us to live our best life serving him. When we submit and commit our ways to him, he promise that he will not withhold no good things from those that love him and walk upright before him. We can't receive the things of God living like the devil. There's a price we must pay. If Jesus had to suffer, we must arm ourselves likewise. I'm a witness that serving the *Lord* will pay off. Stay faithful and committed to "*him.*"

CHAPTER 18

Grateful for God's Grace and Mercy Part 2

I'm by no means an expert on relationships, nor do I proclaim to be. I am an expert by experience. I found that experience is the best lesson a person can be taught, at least for me it was. I know what it is to be saved, sanctified, Holy Ghost-filled, but falling short of God's glory. I know what it feels like to sin and to praise God, feeling like I had weights on my feet.

Sin is nothing but weights, and you cannot praise God with weights on. Can you imagine lifting up heavy weights and trying to run with them? Of course not, it's going to be almost impossible. The same way it's impossible to please God in our "*mess.*" I've been there, done that. God gets no glory when we offer up a stinky sacrifice before *him*. Our sin stinks in God's nostrils.

Thank God, for a spirit of conviction. I tell you the Holy Ghost will convict you of "*sin.*" It's up to us to "*repent*" and turn from our sinful state. I learned when the hands of God is upon' your life, you cannot get away. He'll allow you to go so far, then "he" has a way of rearing us back to our rightful place. It's up to us to take heed to the Holy Ghost when it speaks.

The worst thing for me was to go to church and watch the saints praise God all around me, while I no longer felt the presence of God. *Wow*, that's the worst feeling I could ever experience. I felt as though God's presence had left me. I do know where "sin" abides, God holy spirit does not dwell.

To not feel or experience the presence of God was unbearable for me. I wanted and needed God more than I needed to appease my *"flesh."* I couldn't continue in my mess. I had to confess that thing unto God and repent, asking God for *"his"* forgiveness for my sin.

I learned a valuable lesson, no one is exempted when it comes to the devil. He comes as a roaring lion seeking whom he can devour. He sits and he strategically plots how he's gonna ambush the saints of God. He comes at a time when we're no longer praying and watching. He's not gonna attack as long as we're seeking God. But he sits, and listens, and studies the routine of the saints. He knows when you get slack seeking God, that's his opportunity to come in and draw you away from the faith.

I was under a strict apostolic church, where we weren't allowed to wear pants, jewelry, or makeup. We weren't allowed to date, or go to movies, and our dresses had to be a certain length. We were taught holiness carries a standard, and we just couldn't do whatever we wanted. My life was no longer the same. I served faithfully under this ministry. I loved God and I wanted to be saved for real. I was serious about my walk with Christ. I knew the call of God was upon my life. This church was my foundation. I was under the leadership of a woman pastor. I was taught about sanctification and holiness. But I later learned it wasn't about my outer appearance, because God weighs and searches the heart of man.

Over twenty something years later, God transitioned me from this church where I served faithfully. It was during this time of my transitioning that the enemy was waiting to ambush me. As I stated previously, I met a guy I used to date in high school, we ended up changing phone numbers, and the rest is history as they say. That devil set me up real good, I didn't see that coming. I hadn't dated in years, you see the devil attacks when you're vulnerable, lonely, or when you're off from under a covering. That's his opportunity to make you take down everything you stand or stood for. I thank God for his grace and mercy. Don't be fooled, we are no match for the "enemy."

CHAPTER 19

Warning Signs, "Don't Lose Your Focus"

The devil doesn't care about us coming to church, jumping, shouting, and praising God. He awaits the opportunity to catch you when you're no longer on fire for God. You've gone from being on fire to becoming lukewarm. Why? Anytime you become slack in your prayer life, reading, and meditating on the word of God, you will begin obeying the flesh. Make no mistake; you will know when you're no longer walking in the spirit. Now, you are indulging in the things of the world. All the devil needs is an opening to enter into your idle mind to set up shop. His intention is to rob you of everything that has been sown into you spiritually.

People that were once truly on fire for God act as if they've never been saved. They lost that zeal. The enemy has sucked everything spiritually out of them to the point they act and dress like the world. God told us to put a difference between the clean and unclean things. If you're not grounded and rooted in the word of God, the devil will uproot you. When planting flowers, you have to make sure that flower is rooted properly down in the soil. If it's not planted properly, it will not catch root or it can easily be uprooted. The same thing holds true for the saints of God. If we don't stand for something, we'll fall for anything. We must be steadfast, unmovable in the faith. God has called us to be bold soldiers in his army. We got to be suited up spiritually. God says to put on the whole armor of God that we will be able to stand against the wiles of the devil. We must protect ourselves against Satan's subtle tactics by putting on the helmet of salvation, the breast plate of righteousness, the truth girdle about our loins, and our feet shod on the preparation of the gospel of peace. Having the shield of faith, quenching the fiery darts of the enemy (Ephesians 6:13–17, KJV).

Get suited up!

CHAPTER 20

My Confession, My Truth

We've all fallen from God's grace one time or another since we've been saved, I must admit, this has been my truth. You see I can't tell anyone that God can and will restore you unless he has done it for me first. I'm a witness that he will restore and receive you back unto himself as though you never left. But you must be willing to confess your faults, "repent," and turn from your wicked ways. God is not like man. "Praise God!" He doesn't beat us up with our past. Once we repent and turn from our wrong doings, God puts it in the seat of forgiveness and he remembers not our sins anymore. If you don't know God and what his word tells us concerning repentance, the devil will cause us to hold on to something God has already forgiven us from. We must learn to forgive ourselves and not allow the enemy to beat us up with guilt and shame. With God, there's nothing we can do that's too bad or good that our God won't *"love"* us. Aren't you glad about it?

God loves us so much. Just as a father in the natural that chastises his disobedient child, so will our heavenly Father chastise his disobedient children. You see, *he* loves you and me too much to watch us go astray. God has a way of whipping us without a belt. Trust me, I know, and anybody that has witnessed this experience from God can identify.

I remember when I was seeking an answer from God on whether or not I should marry. God already allowed me to see all the red flags, I obviously overlooked. I remember the man that asked me to marry him was all of a sudden adamant about me marrying him. Although I had my reservations about marrying this man, a part of me still wanted to marry him.

CHAPTER 21

My Confession, My Truth Part 2

I remember sitting in the living room of my apartment one Wednesday evening. I began asking God, "What shall I do?"

The Lord said to me, "Get up, go to Bible study. I'm going to give you the answer through the man of God."

I remember, one of my best friends had called me before leaving for Bible study. I began to share with my friend Gwen what I believed the Lord had spoken to me. So, I left home, went to Bible study, and we were having services in one of the rooms at the YMCA. When I arrived at the "Y," where services were being held, three Caucasian women came down from Birmingham, Al. My pastor at that time was ministering unto these women. Later he said, "We're going to close soon." And, I'm saying within myself, *Lord, I know what you said to me.* We all stood to be dismissed. While going outside, my friend and I were just standing and waiting because I knew what God had spoken.

All of a sudden, our pastor was coming out of the building to get into his van. He then detoured over to where my friend Gwen and I were standing.

He said to me, "Somebody has asked you to marry them."

I replied, "Praise God."

Pastor said, "Can I tell you something? You asked God for this?"

I replied, "Yes, sir."

He said, "Sis. Cal, this man is not your husband. Sis. Cal, one woman is not enough for him, you deserve better than that. Woman, if you wait on God, the man God has for you will treat you like a jewel."

When he got done giving me the word of God, he got into his van.

God affirmed for me just what he said he would do. Knowing what God had already revealed unto me through "*his*" man of God, yet I still disobeyed God.

Lord have mercy.

CHAPTER 22

My Confession, My Truth

Yes, you heard me correctly, I still disobeyed my God knowing what I knew going into the marriage. If I can be honest right here, the minute I said, "I *do*," I promise you it was like a spirit of sorrow immediately came over me. I wasn't happy. I wasn't jumping up and down with joy. The question I asked was "What have I done?" Seriously, I remember coming home from the justice of peace just crying. I never felt so unhappy in my life. I had disobeyed God, number one, I felt like I was being whipped real good by God, and he didn't need a belt.

I was most miserable. I had to smile when my heart was breaking on the inside. Anytime we disobey God, especially when "*he*" has already warned us not to do a thing, we're asking for trouble. Why? Because I didn't enter into it blind. Whatever red flag you see before marriage, you will see during the marriage. In fact it seems as though they become worst or it could be they feel that they now have you. They're just being who they were all the time.

You see, although God granted my request concerning whether or not I should marry this man, I went against the grain. In other words, I knowingly disobeyed God. It wasn't that God didn't know already that I would disobey "*him.*" God will not tempt us, *he* will certainly test us to see where our loyalty for him lies. It also allowed me to see just how far Satan had turned my heart from God. There's a dear price you pay when you walk in the spirit of disobedience.

God truly warned me, but I failed to heed the warning of God. And because of that I went through utter hell in my marriage. But I had to go through it because I knew well what I was getting into, and the lies, the deceit, the infidelity just got worse.

CHAPTER 23

My Confession, My Truth

And the crazy thing about this situation, it wasn't that I didn't know how this man was already because I did. We dated years during high school and afterward. I was not saved during this time and I definitely wasn't the girl that sat around hoping that he will call. Things I tolerated in my marriage with him, trust me, I did not tolerate when I was in the world. Sin will blind you to the point that you somehow settle and tolerate the crap these whorish men do. Let's be clear, I believe there are some godly, saved, single men that are out there somewhere. I just haven't met him yet. But when you marry or date someone that's not saved, you already know you are asking for trouble. Please, don't be naive with the concept that you can change that man. Absolutely not. That man gotta want to change, and it takes God to change an individual, not us.

God is so good, "*he*" doesn't make us serve him, he gives us a choice. Regardless of what I did or could have done, it wasn't enough. People deal with all sorts of addictions, and unless a person gets delivered from that thing, they are literally bound to it. Sometimes they don't know why they do what they do. It's a spirit that they somehow mimic from the daddy or mother side. It's a known fact if a son never witnessed a father being loving to his mother, or having witnessed his mother be disrespected, by the father having affairs with other women. There's a saying that goes, "The apple doesn't fall far from the tree." The same holds true for a woman, you can't give love to a man if you never experienced it growing up. That's why some girls grow up being drug addicts, being promiscuous, at a young age. Why? Because they lacked a mother or a father's love growing up. A lot of young girls fall in love with the attention they get from that man.

Unfortunately, the wrong kind of attention can lead them down a wrong or dangerous path.

CHAPTER 24

My Confession, My Truth

I thank God I was blessed to have two wonderful parents in my home growing up. I never witnessed my dad be disrespectful to my mom or his children as I was growing up. Honest to God, I never heard my dad use profanity in or out of the home, not around his children.

My dad would work two jobs to provide for us so that we would have food on the table. It would bother him to know we wanted or needed something he wasn't able to provide. My dad worked hard in order to provide for seven children. I always would tell myself that when I grow up I was going to marry a man like my dad. Oh, how that devil made a liar out of me.

My mom was a very strict disciplinarian. Now, my mom was short in stature, she was about 5'2, or 5'4, but she walked heavy. She did not play. We knew when she told us to do something, we best to do it. Now, my mom would use a few choice words when she got angry.

But, we knew she meant business. I used to think she was so mean growing up, but her strict discipline kept our butts out of jail. Unlike this generation today, we wouldn't dare tell our parents what we don't feel like doing, if we did we best murmur it under our breath and live.

I gave you a little background history of where I came from. I was blessed to have both parents growing up in the home. My dad died when I was nineteen years old. My mom died in 2014.

She vowed that she would never remarry after our dad died in 1978, and she kept her vow up until God called her home. Oh, how I thank God for our parents. He gave us the best!

Now, how in the world did I manage to hook up with two different men, their family backgrounds were similar. *My* son's daddy was living at home with his mother with an absent dad in his life. So did the man I married, who currently lives at home with his mother and also had an absent father in his life. So, I believe a lot of the behavior they exhibited derived from not having a father figure in the home.

CHAPTER 25

My Confession, My Truth

A mother "nourishes" her children, but a good father shapes and molds his son into the man he is destined to be. A father just doesn't tell his son what type of man he needs to be, he leads by example. Children love their parents, and they trust them, and they watch how they interact with each other. Whether, it is in a good way or bad way, children sometimes imitate the lifestyle they witnessed growing up.

That's not the case with all young men. There are men that were raised by single women and they are intelligent men. Men that actually know how to treat a woman. It takes a good mother with good morals to instill those same values in her children.

Through my experience, I'll tell any saved women, or young ladies, before you start dating, becoming serious about a man or young man, do a background check. Ask questions, find out who his parents are, talk with his siblings if he has any, or his friends. Get a feel of who he is, not who he says he is. If he becomes defensive or reluctant about you asking questions, or maybe meeting his parents, leave that fish right in that pond, honey. You don't need him! Cause whatever secrets he's trying to conceal while you're dating will be "*revealed*" once you marry.

You all better hear what I'm saying. Pay attention to the "warning signs." Please don't ignore all the red flags that are waving out at you. Usually when your spirit gives you a hint that something's not right, *trust it*! Don't wait until it's too late, then here you go. "Girl, I felt like he wasn't being truthful." No, you chose to turn your head the other way. God will warn us when a person is not legitimate or whether they have another agenda concerning you. "*Pay attention*."

CHAPTER 26

My Confession, My Truth

Every flag waved my way, I chose to ignore it. Being young, naive, trustworthy, a lot of things I learned the hard way. The first serious relationship I had was with my son's dad. He ended up being very abusive to me, along with the alcohol and drugs. I tolerated that behavior for years, until I finally came to the conclusion I didn't want to continue living that way. I could not risk my son growing up with the concept that's the way a woman should be treated.

After years of being with this man, I finally had to close the door on that relationship. It had become toxic, I couldn't do it anymore. It's hard to be in a relationship with somebody that wants to control you by abusing you. Not to mention the lies, deceit, and affairs that occurred. I wasn't married to him, but we lived together in sin for years. They called it shacking. I wasn't saved during this time and I don't recommend it to anyone. *Marry!* "Marriage is honorable in all, and the bed undefiled, but whoremongers, and adulterers, God will judge" (Hebrews 13:4, KJV). In other words, marriage should be honored by all and the marriage bed kept pure. Your bed should be your husband's and your sanctuary. Keeping your bed undefiled means no outside activities, extra-marital affairs. Keep it holy.

Years later, I'm saved and married, but I married a man with similar behaviors, lies, deceit, and constant cheating. You would think I had enough. He wasn't physically abusive, but a lot of times verbally. A lot of times verbal abuse hurts just as bad as physical abuse. I repeated this cycle because I still had the residue of my past on me. The residue I yet had on me from my son's daddy identified with the same spirits my ex-husband had. It was like a carry over, the only difference was my ex-husband didn't do hard drugs, he had a good paying job, and he worked and helped take care of the home.

CHAPTER 27

My Confession, My Truth

But who wants an unfaithful spouse, you can't trust? Lies and deceit. I came to realize I kept making poor choices because I had very little confidence in myself. If I could just be real, but I allowed the enemy to convince me that nobody that had some potentials, or really had something going for themselves, would want me. I suffered really low self-esteem, didn't feel like I was pretty, didn't feel like I had anything to offer to a man that really had morals. "*All lies of the enemy.*" I had to go through hell and back with this man to come to the conclusion that enough was enough.

I had to love myself enough to say, "I'm not doing this anymore, I am tired. I had it with all the lies, constant infidelity." Married, but for years I felt as though I was single. *Sin* will blind you. Only when the blinders come off are you able to see. Don't let this be your story.

I hoped he would change. Not. I was determined he wasn't going to pull me into his lifestyle and he was adamant, I wasn't going to change him. *So,* I kept going to church, he continued to be unfaithful. But again, I made that choice. He didn't hold me hostage saying marry me or else.

I did that of my own free will, even when God said he's not the one. So, what I went through with this marriage, I caused upon myself by being disobedient. The first seven years was probably the worst, out of the fourteen years we were actually married. I tell you it's easy to love someone that is lovable, but it's hard to love someone that's not. I had to pray and pray hard. At times, I literally despised that man and if the truth be told, there were times God knows I felt like I could kill him because I was so disrespected I felt bitter and angry. I wanted out!

CHAPTER 28

My Confession, My Truth

I'm being real, is it right? Of course not. Is it real what I felt? Absolutely. There are those men that can bring out the worse and there are some men that bring out the best in a woman.

Well, by now you already know what category I fell into. Don't get me wrong, I wasn't cursing and throwing stuff at him although, I felt like sometimes reverting back to that old nature. Instead I'll shut down to avoid argument or just leave the house before he got home cause I just didn't want to be there. I'm just being real. Sometimes we have to help other people by opening up old wounds so that others can be healed. Maybe somebody reading this can identify with what I was feeling during that time. I refuse to go into details of all I went through, I just praise God that he took me through it. I get it, some might think, well why didn't you just get a divorce?

Beloved, this was my whipping for disobeying God. I had to go through it. I believe if I had not gone through this experience, I would not have learned anything about myself. I would get into the same kind of relationship, "*settling.*" Now, I don't have to. I refuse to anymore...

I'm really feeling good about myself now. I know God has greater plans for me. I just gotta trust and keep my confidence in "*him.*" I'm learning to allow God to work on me. I don't want my next husband to pay for what I went through with my ex. So whatever I'm asking God to give me in a saved mate, I want to give to my mate as well, and more. I thank God. It's by his grace that he has kept me these seven years since my divorce in 2011. I give him all the praise. I've not dated since then and I have remained celibate, praise God. I'm preparing myself for my God-*ordained* husband. He is worth the wait and so am I. Thank God for everything he allowed to go through, as it made me a better me.

CHAPTER 29

My Confession, My Truth

I can look back on my life now and truly thank God for delivering me. For allowing me to see that what I thought I needed actually needed me. Some men don't realize how good they have it until they no longer have it. When our husbands would be unfaithful, we as women have a tendency to question what did I do wrong? The truth of the matter is I don't care what I would have done, he still would have cheated. He had a whoremonger spirit. One time I asked why he does what he does, he replied that he didn't know. Whenever he cheated, it was with young trashy-looking women. I couldn't understand that. I understood later why he targeted those types of females. He needed somebody to control and give into his sexual appetite. Regardless of how I forgave him, he'll stop for a while, and then he would continue that same behavior. I soon had little to no respect for him. I felt I had a roommate rather than a husband.

My marriage was doomed from the beginning. God told me he wasn't my husband, but I married him anyway. It *doesn't* pay to disobey God, there are consequences to pay, trust me.

I remained faithful to him the fourteen years plus. We separated for five or six years, I stayed faithful. He was still doing what he does. Because of my love for God, I had to remain faithful. It was nothing about him, for me it was all about my God. I stayed faithful for fourteen years.

I thank God for what he allowed me to go through. It didn't break me, it made me instead. I was given the green light to file for divorce, that's what I did. God had to make sure when he delivered me that my wounds were healed and I was truly over my ex and his foolishness. Truly, I had had enough. God saw my commitment and faithfulness. Thank you, Jesus!

CHAPTER 30

My Confession, My Truth

You cannot take a person where they aren't ready to go, that was a word the Lord had spoken to me concerning my ex. I would go to church many times, visualizing my husband being in church with me. I would invite him, but at the end of the day it had to be his choice. I must say, after quite some time he did attend church with me a few times. It actually felt good to have my husband to finally attend church with me. Unfortunately, he went with me one Sunday, after the message, there was altar call for those who wanted prayer. He said to me, "I want prayer." Of course, I got up and went to the front with him. I was glad to hear he wanted prayer, but it didn't happen. We both went and sat down, he was discouraged, frankly so was I. But that's water under the bridge. I hope and pray that he will one day become saved, after all Jesus loves him too.

Some people ask me, would I remarry my ex again. Absolutely not! First and foremost, he's not ready for change. He is quick to tell you he's already saved. My prayer for him, is that he be saved, and delivered, so he can learn how to be faithful to one woman. I'm sure men like that don't want to be whorish all their lives. And you have some men just addicted to sex, it has nothing to do with you. It's a stronghold that comes from either the mother or father's side. It's called a generational curse, we have the choice to not allow what affected our parents to affect us, period. People deal with all sorts of generational curse's, such as abuse, drug addictions, alcohol, adultery, depression, being a blatant liar. That doesn't necessarily have to be your story.

Decree the word of God over your life, speak what the word of God says concerning you.

CHAPTER 31

My Confession, My Truth

Our words have power, we have whatsoever we say. If you tell yourself you will never get married or re-marry, then you won't. We must trust and believe that God has a mate for each of us. It's imperative that we, as women of God, must learn to wait upon God.

Unfortunately, that's the thing we as saved women don't want to do. Because God don't send us a mate at the allotted time, we feel we should have one, we handpick our own. We wonder why there are so many failed marriages, in and out of churches. We don't acknowledge God or seek God to find out whether or not that mate is truly ours. I'm a witness that if we pray earnestly asking God, he will answer you. Be prepared for the answer God gives you, it may not be the answer you are hoping for. When God says no, we must understand that he knows what's best for each of us.

After all, we were all created in his likeness, we are his creation, and he is our creator. I learn to trust God, he knows what's best concerning my life. I tried it my way, my way didn't work.

The man I chose to marry wasn't God's choice for me. I never told anyone that God gave me my ex-husband because he didn't. This was absolutely my doing. I disobeyed the Holy Ghost and as a result of my disobedience I went through, praise God, I had to suffer through it because I knew better. It was flesh, not God. What God joins together, let no man put asunder. Does that mean a marriage that is ordained by God won't have problems? Absolutely, *you* will. But when a marriage is ordained by God, you can go through hell and high water, God will see you through any storm. I'm very much encouraged, I believe God has a mate specifically for me.

After going through what I went through, I am determined to wait upon God to bless me with my God-ordained suitor. If that means denying my "flesh" to get what I need from God, so be it!

CHAPTER 32

My Confession, My Truth

In order to get what we desire from the Lord, it costs a price. We must be willing to suffer by denying this flesh and not caving into what this flesh craves for. The flesh, that human nature, we all have. According to the word of God, no good thing dwells in this flesh. We can't please God walking in the flesh. "For they that are after the flesh do mind the things of the flesh; but they that are after the Spirit the things of the Spirit" (Romans 8:5, KJV). Beloved, anytime you walk in the flesh, you're gonna find yourself doing the things contrary to the will of God. When we walk in the spirit, even though your flesh has desires, because of your love for God you choose not to "yield." That's why we have a war that goes on in our members: the flesh versus the spirit.

They're contrary to one another. It's important that we keep our spirit fed with the "Word of God." If we fail to pray, meditate on God's word, on a daily basis, we'll soon start appeasing the flesh. How do you know? Because now your mind is becoming carnal, you begin acting and behaving like the world. This is why we as believers end up making wrong or bad choices.

Whomever we choose to serve and obey, that's who we become a servant to. We cannot serve God and the devil too. You can do it, but God gets no glory. God doesn't want part of us, but all of us. This is why God is so good that he doesn't make us serve him, he gives us a choice.

> Elijah stood in front of them (the peoples), and said, "How much longer will you try to have things both ways? If the *Lord* is God, worship him! But if Baal is your God, worship him!" The people did not say a word. (1 Kings 18:21, Contemporary English Version)

This very thing is occurring with this generation of today, we are still being "halted" between two opinions. You wonder why your blessings are held up, check out your commitment with God. You can't serve two masters.

CHAPTER 33

Delight Yourself in the Lord

If we as believers would learn how to "wait" on God, as we delight ourselves in him, he'll give us the desires of our heart (Psalm 37:4, *New American Standard Bible*). Serving, God is not meant to make us believers feel as though we're in bondage or captivity. When God saved us he made us each free from the yoke of bondage. We should no longer be bound by those things that God has delivered us from. God tells us not to be entangled with the yoke of bondage again. Stay free. Unfortunately, some believers are like recovering addicts. They insist on hanging around those same addicts while recovering. You can't do that, not while you're trying to recover. You are not strong enough yet. That's how it is with some believers, you got to be willing to wait upon God. Allow him to perfect you for whom he has predestined you to be. We can avoid a lot of pitfalls if we will just delight ourselves in "him."

That word delight means to please someone greatly or to take great pleasure in something or someone. I believe the way we please God is to obey his Word. God has promised us if we delight (please) him, he'll give us the desires of our heart. God does not lie. If God said it shall not, he make it good. That's the word of the Lord. Beloved, we just don't get the blessings of God anyhow, it comes with conditions. Yes ma'am and yes sir, we must deny ourselves, take up our cross, and follow him. In other words, you got to be willing to suffer. If Christ suffered, we must arm ourselves likewise. That's the "Word of God." It's called a denied life.

We want the blessings of God yet we don't want to go through anything. Living for God is not hard. It only becomes hard if you're not willing to fully surrender unto the *Lord*. You must have a made up mind. No good thing will he withhold from those who walk uprightly (Psalm 84:11).

CHAPTER 34

Delight Yourself in the Lord Part 2

I've come to realize that we as children of the "Most High God" has so many spiritual benefits serving the *Lord*. Since I have been saved, I've grown to really love God. I love God to the point that I don't want to do anything to hurt him. It's called intimacy. God wants an intimate relationship with us. Ain't nothing like getting in the presence of my God. It becomes personal, and that's why I don't mind waiting upon the *Lord*. Is it easy? No, but it's worth it, and I know my waiting is going to pay off. Why? Because I choose to believe God's word.

    I tried it my way several years ago, and my way wasn't God's way. Doing it our way can cause us to fall away from the faith. The Bible says there is a way that seems right unto a man, but the way thereof is death. Our ways are not God's ways, neither are our thoughts. His (God) ways are higher than the heaven is the earth (Isaiah 55:8). So, we gotta stop thinking we can do contrary to God's word and think it's okay. It's not okay, saints! There is a penalty for *sin*. Some leaders don't want to preach on *sin*. But God said, "Cry loud, spare not," and that's exactly what he means. It's time out for sugar coating the "Word of God." It's time to return back unto our first "love," Christ

Jesus. God's word has not, nor will it change for me or you. It's disturbing how the church is embracing so much of the world's tactics. People don't seem to have the fear of God anymore. We embrace stuff that's not even godly. We're making wrong right and right wrong. What's the matter, church? Nobody's really getting saved because some of our lives are so raggedy, the sinners can't see any difference. We are too busy trying to live like the devil, the reason we can't flourish in God.

CHAPTER 35

Delight Yourself in the Lord

God doesn't want part of us, he wants all of us. He (God) wants to be first or nothing at all. God is a jealous God. He doesn't want us putting anything before him. God loves you and I just that much. Do you not know Jesus styled the church as "his bride?" So, when our focus becomes solely on trying to please our flesh rather than "him," then God becomes displeased.

We must seek ye first the kingdom of God and his righteousness, and all these other things shall be added unto you (Matthew 6:33, KJV). It's not that God doesn't want us blessed with the desires of our heart but he wants us to spend time with "*him*" and become intimate with "*him*."

God wants to be the apple of our eyes. The same should hold true for us being the children of the Most High God.

God needs to know that when he does bless us with a God-ordained suitor, you and I will stay "committed" unto "*him*." Beloved, God will not bless us with something that's going to take us away from "*him*." We just don't receive the blessing of God, living and doing whatever we want. No, Ma'am! We must be willing to suffer for the name of "*Jesus*."

Even if it means waiting years, God knows what it takes for each of us. I know we may feel sometimes that we are ready for marriage.

The truth of the matter is some of us haven't stopped fornicating. Some of us still dealing with a lustful spirit, the reason we can't submit to God. You feel you got to have you a man, that's your whole focus. Not realizing that the more you choose to be unfaithful to God, the longer your blessing will be held up. We don't receive the blessing of God living like the devil. To please God, deny your flesh. Don't yield to the "cravings."

CHAPTER 36

Don't Be Tricked, Fooled, or Deceived by the Enemy

Woman of God, know your self-worth, know that you are valued by the *Lord*. He (God) loves us too much to allow us to be tricked, fooled, or deceived by the enemy. The devil is a liar! He's an impostor and a deceiver. It's important today that we ask God to sharpen our discernment. We must be able to discern the things of God. There are people in sheep's clothing, but inwardly they are ravening wolves. Remember, when we pray to God concerning the kind of mate we desire, the enemy listens as well. When we pray, we must trust God with all our heart. He knows the things concerning us. After all, did he not create each of us?

You know being in two failed relationships, the devil would tell me that a good man wouldn't want me. Why? Because the enemy would make me feel like I wasn't pretty enough or I wasn't smart enough for an intelligent man. Lies of the enemy, I realize that now. I dealt with poor self-esteem. I was my worst critic. Regardless if someone gave me a compliment, I would have something negative to say. This is why I think I settled when it came to certain men. Not that these men were so terrible, but I realize now that they just weren't worthy of me. I can truly say that now.

That's why I'm finally at a place in my life that I only want who God has for me. I love "me."

I now realize before I can truly love someone, I must learn to love me first. Be willing to make yourself happy. Take yourself on a vacation, tell yourself you look good. You don't need to be, "*validated*." Know who you are in Christ Jesus. Know what he says about you, according to his word. Don't listen to the lies of the enemy concerning you or your future.

I appreciate God for everything he allowed me to go through. Had I not gone through my experience, I would *not* have the mindset I now have. I believe everything that happens has a purpose. And every experience we should learn from. Unfortunately, that's not every woman's story. Some women feel they just have to have them a man and for what? Just to say you have somebody? Don't give your soul to the devil. You are so much more valuable than you know.

Ask God to help you to start preparing yourself for your God-ordained suitor. Remember, just as you're praying for a saved mate, there's a saved man asking God for a saved wife as well.

We must be in a place and a position with God that we are sensitive to the voice of God.

God knows how to set us up. There's a time and a season for all things. In due time, God is gonna blow your mind. Stay faithful, regardless of how long you've been waiting. If you are not married yet, know there's a reason. Sometimes God has to deliver us from some things we are trying to hold on to. Sometimes it can be simply "*unforgiveness*" from past relationships.

Nevertheless, God knows what it takes for each of us, we just gotta "trust him!"

I don't know about you but I desire a mate that will see my heart and not "flesh." A man of God that can smell the fragrance of my anointing and can cover me in the "Spirit." Not only do I want him to cover me, but that I cover him as well. Why? Because we are one, we are a team, and a team sticks together. So while you wait on your God-ordained suitor, spend time with your God, get acquainted with "*him*," spend time in the "Word of God. Put God first!

THE DANGER OF NOT WAITING ON GOD

Once God sees our faithfulness and commitment, then I believe, he will release us to our mates.

God is not going to bless us with a mate, only to have us turn our backs on "*him*." That's not going to happen, he's a jealous God. So while you wait, ask God to help you work on you. Go back to school, do something you have desired to do but just haven't taken the time to do so. Just don't become "idle," but challenge yourself to do something you've never done. Enjoy being single while you can.

I know some of you are anxious to get married, for whatever reason. Time and age is nothing to God. He knows our beginning and our ending. I think sometimes we forget that God is our creator; nothing surprises "*him*" concerning us. Where we are today, God has already been. God knows those of us that are single, those who desire a husband or wife.

In fact, he has each of our mates already chosen that we just got to wait upon him or her. Now ask yourself, are you worth the wait? Better yet, are you willing to wait? Let God give us what we need. It doesn't matter with God how old you are or how long you been waiting. God is so God, he's able to catapult us where we need to be, he's that kind of God. I choose to trust and wait upon Him. Remember tall, and special orders take time.

Don't allow the enemy to deceive you, *stay* in the will of your heavenly Father. Don't sell out to the devil because your flesh is burning. Stay off your back, get on your knees and cry out to your God. He already knows your struggles, your weakness. Don't be ashamed to ask God to strengthen you where you are weak. He already knows. He wants us to call upon *him*.

Seek "*his*" face, ask for "*his*" guidance concerning your life. God doesn't want us walking in error or sin. He gives us a way of escape. We don't have to fall prey to the devil, only when we're not watching and praying. So if you happen to venture off straight street, stop, turn around, and get back on the right road. God has brought you too far to allow the enemy to deceive you not to wait on God. Keep in mind, when God is getting ready to bless your life, the enemy comes with all sorts of attack. Anytime, you say to yourself, "*Lord,* what is going on? Looks like everything, except the kitchen sink, is falling apart." Know that's the enemy trying to get you, out of position. Oppositions is a indication you are in the right position. Don't be moved! Your blessing is on the way.

CHAPTER 37

In Conclusion, Don't Forfeit Your Blessing

"For moments of pleasures."

Good things come to those who wait upon the Lord. The key word here, ladies, is wait, upon "*him*" and he (God) shall give us the desires of our hearts. He promises that he will not withhold no good things from those who love him and walk upright before "*him*" (Psalm 84:11).

It is imperative that we know what the "Word of God" says. We can remind God of his word. Why? Because God honors his word. He says in the Word of God, if I said it, shall not I *do it*. Just in case you don't know, God is faithful to his Word. The Bible is like our manual, anything we need to know it's in the word of God." Don't become weary in well doing, for in due season you will reap, if you faint not (Galatians 6:9, KJV).

Each of us has a scheduled time with God to be blessed. God honors our commitment and faithfulness unto "*him*." Do not forfeit your blessing "to the devil" for a few minutes of pleasures. God has so much more for "*his*" children. The enemy knows who you are. Keep in mind he was once an angel of light. So his (the devil's) agenda is to get you out of the will of God. It's our responsibility to be steadfast, unmovable in the *Lord*. You gotta know, whatever God has promised it shall come to pass. Don't be overtaken by the "*lies*" of the enemy. He is the father of lies. "There is no truth in him!" He (God) knows how to expedite our lives.

Did not God say a thousand years with "*him*" is like one day? We must cast the lies of the devil down. Remind him of what your God says concerning your future. Listen, trust me, I know it's not easy, it's a struggle for us single, saved ladies. But when you truly have the love of God in your heart, pleasing "*him*" is more important than trying to please the "*flesh*."

That's part of the "*intimacy*" between you and your God. Imagine a wife that has a husband or a husband that has a wife, if they truly love each other they're not gonna do anything to jeopardize their union. We must resist the temptations of the enemy. Resist the devil and he shall flee. You must first submit yourselves to God (James 4:7, KJV). We must come under God's authority. The only reason we don't do it, we've not denied the flesh. You cannot please God while walking in the flesh. If God had to suffer in the flesh, we must arm ourselves likewise.

Again, it's called "the denied life." We cannot live like the devil and expect God to meet our demands, no ma'am. If we can live like the devil, what's the point in getting saved? You might as well stayed in the world and do like you wanna. There is a standard that God requires from the people of God. People want the blessings of God, but not the one who is responsible for your blessings. God loves us so much there ain't nothing he won't do for his children.

God requires that same love in return. Ask God to help you fall in love with "*him*."

Ask God to help you focus on the things concerning "*him*." God wants to bless us. Of course when he blesses us, he wants us to remain "faithful." Don't risk the danger of not waiting on God by becoming impatient. Don't ignore the warning signs, a warning always comes before destruction. Stay on the street called straight, don't detour or venture off. You don't know what lies ahead of you if you get out of the will of God. Don't get from under the ark of safety, you're too close to the finishing line. Stay in the race, your blessing is nigh. Encourage yourself in the *Lord*. Read and meditate upon the Word of God. Stay prayerful, give yourself unto fasting. What you do privately, God will reward you openly. There are benefits, beloved, in serving our God. We must be patient and trust his Word, for his Word is *"truth."*

I pray that whosoever reads this book be blessed, know we all have weaknesses, we have our struggles. But I declare if you confess whatever you are struggling with unto God, he will deliver you from that stronghold. And, beloved, when God delivers you, be not entangled with the yoke of bondage. Don't go back indulging in what God has set you free from. Whatever is holding you back from your past, let it go! You can't move forward looking backward.

Let God prepare you for your "Boaz," your redeemer. God has a man of God designed or created just for you. Don't *"settle,"* beloved. God has greater plans for your life. Some of you once had a bad marriage or relationship, *wait* patiently on God. He's gonna bless your life with the real deal. Don't give up on relationships because they were unsuccessful. Much like mine's, that was our doing. I tried it my way, now I got to trust God for the mate that he has specifically for me. I'm excited what God is gonna do in my life. I have his assurance because I have remained faithful. I hold fast to God's promises, and so shall you.

My prayer is that God give you your heart's desire and that you don't get weary and give up. I pray your faith be strengthened, and that you seek God with all your heart. Whatever God has promised you, beloved, wait upon it. When your due season comes, he will surely bring it to pass. Press toward the mark of the high calling in "Christ Jesus," forgetting those things that are behind you (in your past). Leave it there! God has a brighter future for both you and I. Believe it! It's according to our faith.

In my conclusion, while you are waiting on God to prepare you for your mate, keep yourself looking good, smelling good in the meantime. Carry yourself like the *"queen"* that you are. You belong to a *"royal"* family. Know who you are in the *Lord*. Don't wait to be "validated."

You've been approved by God, that's all the validation you need. I love you, stay in the faith.

Know that you are on the mind of God. He's not forgotten the things concerning you. Stay with God, he'll stay with you Be Blessed, shalom! (Peace)

ABOUT THE AUTHOR

Carolyn James is a first-time author, licensed minister, mother of one son, and four wonderful grandchildren. She resides in Tuscaloosa, Alabama. Carolyn retired from the Alabama Department of Mental Health and Bryce Hospital, where she served for twenty-six years.

She received her associate degree in biblical studies at American Bible University in Atlanta, Ga. She became a licensed minister under the former leadership of Elder Andrew Turner, founder of Overcoming Deliverance Church of Today in Tuscaloosa, Al.

Ms. James is the second eldest of seven siblings, daughter of the late Edward and Gustava Bonner. Carolyn James is a God-fearing, anointed vessel of God, a woman of faith. Her passion is to inspire, encourage, and motivate the people of God to be all you can be in Christ Jesus.